CW00394408

A history of Bankside, Bermondsey and 'The Borough'

Acknowledgements

Thanks are due to Jennifer Jones for collecting and compiling the text in this booklet. The cost for this work was met by the South Thames Training & Enterprise Council.

In compiling this short history, the publications of "Bankside", "The Borough", and "Bermondsey", were heavily drawn upon. These booklets are produced by the London Borough of Southwark Local Studies Library, and acknowledgement is owed especially to Mary Boast, who wrote the original texts.

We are grateful to Nicola Smith and Stephen Humphrey of the Local Studies Library, for their help in correcting and checking the material, and to both the Local Studies Library and the Illustrated London News for the use of some of their archive material. The 'Old London Bridge' watercolour is reproduced with thanks, from a postcard produced by the Muscular Dystrophy Group.

Special thanks are due to Peter Moore of Pre-Construct Archaeology Limited for providing the text and photographs on the chapter entitled 'Archaeology- discovering a hidden legacy' and to Southwark Cathedral and Southwark Council for the use of their images.

Published by Robert J. Godley in collaboration with Southwark Heritage Association. Printed and produced in England by Robert James (Publications) Ltd 137 Bourne Vale, Bromley, BR2 7NY, in memory of Dan Cullen who first introduced us to Bankside, years ago. Email robjamesdesign@btconnect.com

ISBN No. 0 9528 6442 8

Opposite: *The George Inn, 1881. From a photograph in the Local Studies Library, Borough High Street, London SE1.*

From Skin Market Place, prior to ground-breaking in 1987

'Festival of Firsts' June 1997, the performances begin.

The two inset pictures above are reproduced by kind permission of June Everett, Artist of the Record at the Globe theatre and represent the first and last stages in the story of this ambitious re-construction project.

These watercolours form part of a collection of over 155 paintings known as 'An Eye On The Globe' which graphically describes the story of the re-construction of Shakespeare's Globe Theatre on Bankside.

The oak skeleton,
Shakespeare's Globe reconstruction.
Photo: Richard Kalina

Contents

Shakespeare's Globe 1599 as imagined by a Victorian engraver. Reproduced from a 19th century steel engraving, the wash-colour was almost certainly added during the 20th Century.

Historic Southwark
Foreword

South of the River Thames is not the barren waste of northern nightmares, but rather the historic heartland of the capital's thriving life.

Here in Southwark, great themes of the nation's long history have run, from the arrival of the Romans to the depressing decay of the docks and industry, swiftly followed by yet another renaissance in commercial activity, another recession, and another struggle for growth and regeneration.

To cross London Bridge and stand at the end of Borough High Street and look about, is to absorb in that one panoramic sweep more than could be learned from a thousand history lessons. All London life, high born or low, had to cross that bridge, or one of its predecessors, in order to trade, to travel, to be entertained, or imprisoned for debt, death, or martyrdom. Southwark was not the melting pot of kings and courtiers, wealth and power, but rather the cauldron where was stirred the infinitely variable ingredients of trade, commerce, and money making skills so vital if wars were to be fought, and great visions made reality for the global power that Britain once was.

It was the Romans with their incredible engineering skills, who created Southwark. They came and found three separate, sandy islands bordered by a riverside of mud and marsh.

Their road-builders bridged the gaps between the islands, draining the water before laying a foundation of timber logs to carry a firm road surface. And they built a strong wooden bridge.

Wealthy Romans came to live in this suburb across the river from the City of Londinium, leaving their detritus for our archaeologists to unearth two thousand years later - mosaic paving, under-floor heating, pots and dishes imported from France, bone needles, hairpins, and statues of their gods.

The Dark Ages took their toll on Southwark. The bridge was broken down and rebuilt several times, until in 1014 it was pulled down by Ethelred, King of England. The marauding Danes had occupied the City and Southwark, and had a strong position on the bridge to ward off the forces of the king and his ally, Olaf of Norway. Olaf made roofs for his ships and sailed them under the bridge, where his men tied ropes to the piers. On command they rowed hard and pulled down the bridge with the Danes on it. London was saved and a rhyme was born:

London Bridge has fallen down, My fair lady.

In medieval times London Bridge was rebuilt in stone. It took thirty years from 1176-1209 to construct the magnificent bridge with its houses, shops, chapel, and a great gate at either end. It lasted for six hundred years and was the only crossing point over the Thames for all the travellers, pilgrims, clergy, merchants, ordinary folk, kings and princes, rebels and traitors, drawn to the great city for their own particular purpose, or to fulfil an unknown destiny.

Because so many travellers used the bridge, the Borough inns grew in number and reputation to provide them with food, drink and a bed for the night. Most of the inns were three-sided around a courtyard with an entrance directly onto Borough High Street. The most famous was the Tabard, where the Canterbury pilgrims gathered; the George, the White Hart, the Queen's Head, and many others of lesser status contributed to Southwark's reputation for providing hospitality and entertainment.

The great Elizabethan age saw the emergence of the theatres on Bankside, and the rise of William Shakespeare. Theatres were banned by the City authorities who refused to grant licences. It was Southwark's good fortune that instead of the City, they set up on Bankside, adding to the noisy, exciting and raffish atmosphere generated by the already existing brothels, women of the 'stews', bear and bull-baiting, bowling, and gambling. In these Bankside theatres - the Rose, the Swan, the Hope, and the Globe, were performed some of the finest plays written in the English language, not just by Shakespeare, but also by Christopher Marlowe and Ben Jonson.

Southwark had established itself as an important commercial centre and reached its zenith during the Victorian era. Its commercial importance continued with the rapid growth of the docks, wharves and warehouses upstream as far as London Bridge, and beyond, after Rennie's new bridge with wider arches made it possible for barges to sail up the river. Hay's Wharf was built in 1856 by William Cubitt for the Hay's Wharf Company, the largest and most powerful of the dockside companies with property all along the river front as far as Tower Bridge. Pickford's warehouses in Clink Street were built in 1864, five storeys high.

Until steamships replaced the sailing vessels, the beautiful clipper ships brought the new season's tea all the way from China to unload at Hay's Wharf. The faster refrigerated ships carried butter and cheese from Australia and New Zealand. Tooley Street, where the warehouses were concentrated, was known as "London's larder".

Other important industries developed: leather working, brewing and the hop trade, printing, broom-making, tin can manufacture. With foodstuffs from all over the world coming into Bermondsey, the Borough, and Bankside, a natural home emerged for processing and packaging firms. Pearce Duff made custard powder, Crosse and Blackwell made pickles, Jacob's biscuits were made in Wolseley Street, Courage's brewed beer and Hartley's produced jams in Tower Bridge Road. The longest surviving company was Peek Frean's in Drummond Road. Near Bankside were factories producing vinegar, biscuit flavourings, and cocoa. Engineering proliferated - Hayward Brothers made the patterned covers for coal holes, Coles produced cranes, while Easton and Amos made the original waterworks for the fountains of Trafalgar Square.

During World War II, Southwark's riverside docks were heavily bombed and huge tracts of buildings destroyed deep into Bermondsey. Far worse, in the eyes of many Southwark people, than the war damage, was the closing down of the docks during the early 1970s. Goods started to be transported in container ships requiring more space and deeper water, not to be found on the river Thames. The warehouses were no longer needed and many were demolished, leaving large open spaces.

In 1980 the St Martin's Property Corporation Limited acquired 27 acres of derelict land which, by 1987 was transformed into 2.7 million square feet of high quality office, retail, residential, leisure, and hospital accommodation. National and international companies moved into the prestigious buildings in London Bridge City, as it became known. Other companies built new premises for themselves, Lloyds Bank at Red Lion Court, and the Midland Bank, a cheque clearing centre, both in Park Street. The Financial Times occupies a building on the river front, at Southwark Bridge, and Sea Containers has converted a building which was conceived originally as an hotel, at Blackfriars Bridge.

At Butler's Wharf, the vision of Sir Terence Conran is slowly nearing completion, though not without setbacks. There too, the old buildings which survived the war and demolition, have been restored to the highest standards, cleaned, and presented anew to the world, much as they would have looked in Victorian times.

The regenerative process has for the most part been made possible by the presence of the London Docklands Development Corporation, armed with the power to speed up planning decisions and to act as a catalyst for developers and visionaries.

Now that Sam Wanamaker's full-size replica of Shakespeare's Globe Theatre on Bankside is finished and open, Southwark's history has finally come full circle.

Beginnings

B *efore the Roman occupation of Britain, the district now known as Southwark would have largely consisted of marsh, with isolated island areas prone to flooding at high tide. There were no bridges across the river and the Thames was very much wider and shallower than it is today.*

There may have been early settlements, and on several sites in north Southwark, pottery and flint tools of the bronze and iron ages have been found.

At a site in Southwark Street evidence has been found of more permanent iron age inhabitation, with flints, pottery and a coin of the period 25BC – AD25.

A grave of a young man, probably from this period, was also found nearby. The first extensive settlement of Southwark, however, began not long after AD43, the year when the Emperor Claudius launched his successful invasion of Britain. In the marshy ground of Southwark the invading Romans found one particular island site to which they could build a

crossing from a hill on the north side of the river. Excavations have shown that north Southwark became a major suburb of Londinium, capital of the Roman province, Britannia.

The first known bridge for what became the city of Londinium was about 20 metres downstream from the modern London Bridge.

The Romans also built wooden retaining walls to control the river channels and other small bridges across the many inlets from the river. Two major roads were constructed, both of which approached the Thames. These roads from the south coast intersected to the south of the bridge, near the present site of the Church of St George the Martyr,

An anthropoid dagger- so called from the face on the pommel- discovered in Stoney Street, Southwark, and ascribed to c.200 bc

Roman remains discovered in Southwark

Stane Street was the road from Chichester and Watling Street came from Dover. It is possible to follow the approximate routes of these roads down Newington Causeway/ Kennington Park Road and along Tabard Street/Old Kent Road respectively. The road across the island to the bridge, once Long Southwark, is now known as Borough High Street.

There is also evidence of another road found below Montague Close, north of the Cathedral, which may have linked two crossing points: the Roman London Bridge and another further upriver at Westminster. The roads were made of gravel, and where they crossed marshy ground, logs were laid as a foundation to prevent the gravel from sinking.

Early findings from around AD50-70 include pottery and coins, and at least one substantial stone building.

The material found compares with that from sites elsewhere in Britain which were known military supply bases. It is thought likely that Southwark was one such base; a staging post in the network for the distribution of men, goods and official communications. Finds of military equipment include bronze fittings and ornaments belonging to soldiers and their horses.

By about AD75 a large suburb was growing up on the south side of the Thames and along the roads leading to it. Under the arches of London Bridge station and also to the west of Borough High St

ROMAN LONDON by Peter Frost

during excavation work for the Jubilee Line extension to the underground network, Archaeologists have discovered considerable evidence of this Roman suburb, including parts of a number of buildings. At least one of the buildings was quite grand with external stone walls and mosaic floors.

Fragments of painted wall plaster, coloured glass mosaic cubes and Italian marble wall and floor veneers found in the buildings indicate that some were richly decorated.

Water was obtained from timber-lined wells, and the discovery of a length of lead pipe suggests that some of the buildings had a direct supply. Little evidence has been found within the buildings to suggest their functions, although some appear to be military, some were certainly warehouses and the majority were probably residential.

During 1995/6 excavation work relating to the extension of the Jubilee underground line has revealed that Southwark was far more significant to the Romans than was previously thought.

Numerous artefacts found have offered insights into the everyday lives of the population. These include oil lamps for lighting, and the vessels they used for cooking and drinking.

Large amounts of butchered animal bones and a variety of seeds reveal much about what the people ate.

Near the end of the 2nd century, the Roman settlement in Southwark, along with the city on the north bank, appears to have entered a period of decline. It recovered in the later years of the 3rd century, although the buildings from this period were of a different character. They were substantial stone structures with underfloor heating systems in some rooms, but it is not yet certain whether they were private homes or used for official purposes.

The evidence for the end of the Roman settlement in Southwark is not clear, but it is thought that the Barbarian invasion of Italy forced the recall of Britannia's legions to Rome's defence in AD 410.

The discovery of a 4th century defensive wall along the riverside of the city might indicate that the population was threatened by sea-borne raiders.

Southwark may then have become unsafe for civilian habitation. Archaeological evidence of the inhabitants during this time is scarce, until the early Norman occupation.

The main picture above shows a late 1st century novelty Roman oil lamp in the shape of a sandalled right foot, discovered during the excavations of the Jubilee Line Extension in 1995/6.

Many items of Roman pottery and amphorae have been discovered in Southwark. Amphorae would have been used for the transportation of wine and produce from far-flung corners of the Roman empire.

Medieval Southwark

Medieval map of Southwark

*T*he Romans occupied Britain for some three hundred and fifty years but there is no evidence of further occupation until after around AD900 when London Bridge was rebuilt.

The first written record of the name Southwark occurs in an early 10th century document known as the 'Burghal Hidage' which contains details of fortifications or 'burghs'. Southwark was known as 'Suthringa Geweorche' meaning Surrey Work, or the defensive works of the people of Surrey. Later it was spelled Sudwerca, - the 'work' to the south of London Bridge.

Southwark appears in the Domesday Book, compiled in 1086, which mentions at least forty households, and a minster or large church, probably on the site where Southwark Cathedral stands today.

By 1295 Southwark was important enough to have two Members of Parliament, the first district in London outside the City to be granted this right.

In 1598 John Stow, the great historian of London, wrote 'The Borough of Southwark... consisteth of divers streets and winding lanes, all full of buildings.'

Further down Borough High Street, opposite the site of St George the Martyr, was Suffolk Place, home of Charles Brandon, the Duke of Suffolk, whose wife Mary was a sister of Henry VIII. At a later date the King took over the building as a mint, remembered today by the name Mint Street.

Long Southwark and London Bridge from a drawing by Wyngaerde

Bermondsey

The parish Church of St Mary Magdalene, Bermondsey St, is the oldest building in Bermondsey. The first Rector was John de Ecclesia in 1291. Much of the church was rebuilt in 1680 and the upper parts including the tower, rebuilt again in 1830.

*T*he modern day Bermondsey was also a low island to the east of Southwark, which rose slightly above the surrounding marshy ground. It was called the Island of Beornmund or 'Beornmund's Eye' after a Saxon lord of that name.

Bermondsey, following the defeat by William the Conqueror, was a royal manor and is mentioned in the Domesday Book.

In 1082 Bermondsey Abbey was founded, dedicated to St Saviour, on the site of a small monastery thought to have dated from around 700AD.

In 1094 William Rufus gave the monks the surrounding manor and later Henry I gave them land in Rotherhithe, Dulwich and Southwark. Henry II spent Christmas 1154 at the Abbey.

In 1117 the monks found a Saxon cross by the Thames which they thought had been dropped from heaven, and many pilgrims subsequently came to worship the Rood of St Saviour.

Following the dissolution by Henry VIII in 1538, the Abbey was bought by Sir Thomas Pope who demolished it after 1541, using the stones to build a mansion for himself known as Bermondsey House. It was later occupied by the Earl of Sussex and it is known that Queen Elizabeth I visited him there.

Today the extent of the inner courtyard of the Abbey can still be seen in Bermondsey Square, and the hinges of the east gate can be found nearby on the wall of a house in Grange Walk.

Now Bermondsey Square is the site of the world famous Bermondsey antique market, which is held every Friday morning.

Bermondsey antique market

The Angel Inn

Situated at 24 Rotherhithe Street, there has been an inn on this site since the 15th century when the monks of Bermondsey Abbey sold their ales here. Formerly known as the Salutation, the name was changed to the Anchor after the Reformation. Samuel Pepys is known to have been a regular visitor, and from here Judge Jeffreys is believed to have watched the hanging of pirates at Execution Dock opposite.

Nearby are the remains of King Edward III *(1327-1377) moated manor house. Built in the mid 1350's and costing £1200, it was one of many royal palaces to be built along the Thames*

Bermondsey Abbey, founded in 1082 was largely demolished by the 19th century. This 19c engraving by N. Whittock owes more to imagination than fact.

The Angel Inn

Right: *High wassail on the frozen Tham Roasting an ox on the ice by old London Bric during the great frost of 15(*

London Bridge

*A*fter the Roman occupation, it is thought that their bridge was broken down by flood or fire and rebuilt several times in wood.

One of these bridges was probably destroyed in 1014 when accounts tell that Ethelred, King of England, with his ally Olaf (or Olave), King of Norway, sailed up the Thames to attack the Danes who had occupied the city and built fortifications in Southwark. The original version of a familiar rhyme, by Norse poet Ottar Svarte, tells the story:

"London Bridge is broken down
Gold is won and bright renown
Shields resounding

War horns sounding
Hildur shouting in the din
Arrows singing
Mailcoats ringing
Odin makes our Olaf win."

The bridge was swept away by a gale in 1091, rebuilt, then destroyed by fire in 1136 and reconstructed once again, this time in elm.

The first stone bridge was begun in 1176 by Peter de Colechurch and took thirty-three years to build.

The bridge had nineteen small arches which restricted the flow of the river and made the current so strong that it was dangerous to go through the arches. Consequently, in severe winters the Thames froze over completely and for many years Londoners held frost fairs on the ice.

An old proverb stated that London Bridge was for wise men to go over and for fools to go under.

The first mention of houses on the bridge was in 1201 and eventually it also had shops and a chapel. Nonsuch House was at the Southwark end and was made entirely of wood secured only with wooden pegs. There was a drawbridge and a large stone gatehouse, upon which the custom of

The frozen Thames - a frost fair

impaling par-boiled, tar-dipped heads upon spikes was begun with that of William Wallace, the Scots patriot.

Other famous heads included Jack Cade, Thomas More and Thomas Cromwell.

This London Bridge was used for over six hundred years and until 1750, when Westminster Bridge was opened, it was the only bridge in the London area.

Between 1823-31 the old London Bridge was demolished and replaced a short distance up river by a new bridge with five stone arches, built by Sir John Rennie. It was opened by William IV and Queen Adelaide on 1 August, 1831.

This bridge existed until 1967 when it was sold, eventually dismantled and re-erected at Lake Havasu, Arizona, U.S.A.

The present pre-stressed concrete structure of three spans was completed in 1972 and utilises the bank-side remnants of the Rennie bridge as huge supports for the roadway. This has created a large enclosed chamber, within which remain the original granite staircases either side of the Rennie bridge. This marriage of convenience may be clearly seen at the westernmost end of Tooley Street.

Until 1928 there was a church to the east of London Bridge called St. Olave's and the name Tooley Street is a corruption of St. Olave's Street.

Left: *Old London Bridge from a water-colour painting attributed to C.T. Dodds.*

Other Bridges

Casting on the old Blackfriars railway bridge.

Blackfriars Bridge, completed in 1769, was the first to be built in Southwark after London Bridge. And Southwark Bridge, made from cast iron, was a toll bridge built in 1819.

Tower Bridge from Potter's Fields, © Southwark Council

It is thought by some, that our use of the expression 'o'clock' possibly dates from about 1797,when a tax on clocks was imposed. In order to obtain the time and avoid the tax, the City institutions would send runners across London Bridge into one of the many inns of Southwark to obtain the time from a large Act of Parliament clock. The runners would then race back over the bridge to their employers in the City, shouting "It's eleven of the clock" etc. The Act was repealed nine months after it was introduced because it was very difficult to enforce, and led to a serious decline in the horological trades.

There is a reference to this in Charles Dickens' novel Little Dorrit when John Chivery put 'His penny on the toll plate of the iron bridge'.

Tower Bridge, opened in 1894 by the Prince and Princess of Wales, was the first bridge to be constructed below London Bridge. Before this time those wanting to travel over the river would take a ferry, landing at Battlebridge Stairs, Pickle Herring Stairs, Horselydown Stairs or Cherry Garden Stairs.

Tower Bridge was designed in a Gothic style by Horace Jones with John Wolfe-Barry as the engineer. Jones' designs were modified after his death in1887 to be more in keeping with the architecture of the Tower of London. In order to allow ships passage through to unload at the wharves further up river, it was designed with opening 'bascules' using steam powered hydraulics. Electrification and oil hydraulics were introduced in 1972.

Tower Bridge is probably the most famous of the bridges and has become one of London's foremost attractions, providing a unique exhibition about the bridge and its construction.

Southwark Bridge

Southwark Inns

The Blue-Eyed Maid,
Borough High Street

*T*he road south of London Bridge became very important as it was the only route south from the City, and a number of inns were established in medieval times to provide food and shelter for those travelling to or from London.

These inns have become celebrated, most notably by Chaucer, who describes in his 'Canterbury Tales' a group of pilgrims travelling from the Tabard Inn to the shrine of St Thomas Becket at Canterbury Cathedral.

The Tabard was only one of a number of inns. John Stow writing in 1598, mentions eight celebrated establishments.

The only one remaining, and the only galleried coaching inn left in London, is The George, built in 1676 on the site of an earlier building.

Below right:
The old 'Tabard' Inn in the 17th century.

Below:
Calvert's Buildings

It originally surrounded three sides of the courtyard but the central and northern wings were demolished in 1899 to make way for buildings associated with the railway. It was taken over by the National Trust in 1937. (See photograph on inside front cover).

There were many other inns here too, including the King's Head, the Queen's Head, the White Hart, the White Lion, the Red Lion, the Nag's Head, the Boar's Head, the Bull's Head and the Blue Eyed Maid. In the 18th century, regular coaches were established, travelling from the inns to all parts of southern England. Each inn was the starting point for a different destination: services from the King's Head included coaches to Dover, from

the White Hart to Portsmouth and Rye, from the Tabard to Chichester, Lewes, Cranbrook, Petworth and Midhurst and from the George to Maidstone, Canterbury, Dover, Brighton and Hastings.

Southwark had a great fire in 1676, ten years after the Great Fire of London, and most of the inns had to be rebuilt, some of which existed well into the 19th century.

The White Hart was the largest of the coaching inns and was demolished in 1889.

It is referred to by Shakespeare in Henry VI and by Dickens as the place where Mr Pickwick first encounters Sam Weller in Pickwick Papers. Dickens also refers to the George in Little Dorrit. The only remaining evidence of these inns is the names of some of the alleyways off Borough High Street: King's Head Yard, White Hart Yard, Talbot Yard (a later name for the Tabard) and Mermaid Court. Between 52 and 54 Borough High Street there is an opening which leads to what was probably the Goat Inn and is now Calvert's Buildings. This area of Southwark escaped the fire in 1676.

Southwark Cathedral

*T**he first building to the west of London Bridge is Southwark Cathedral, the oldest building in Southwark and one of the oldest in London. A £13 million restoration programme was completed in 2001 and includes a state-of-the-art visitor centre, restaurant and shop.***

There has been a church on this site for at least one thousand years. Some say that it was built by St. Swithun, Bishop of Winchester around 852 to 862AD, although the first documentary evidence of the church is in the Domesday Book of 1086. It was rebuilt in 1106 and again a century later, after a fire.

The tower seen today was completed in 1520, and the bells have been recast from those which were rung in 1577 when Queen Elizabeth I attended a wedding nearby.

In the Middle Ages the church was part of the Priory of St Mary Overie (meaning 'over the river' or 'on the river') and was run by Augustinian canons. After the dissolution of the monasteries by Henry VIII the priory church became the parish church of St Saviour.
The cloisters were granted to the father of Lord Montague, the site of which is remembered today as Montague Close.

In the 1830's the nave fell into ruins and the church became known as St Saviour's Folly.

The chapel at the east end was demolished in 1830 during the rebuilding of London Bridge, and in 1897 a new nave was built. In 1905 St Saviour's became the Cathedral for the new diocese of Southwark, which stretches from Richmond in the far west of London to Woolwich in the east and as far south as Reigate in Surrey.

Remnants of the Cathedral's history can still be seen: in the north aisle there are two rounded Norman arches which survived the fire of 1213; at the east end, the choir and retro-choir date from the 13th and 14th centuries, and the carved stone screen behind the high altar was presented by Richard Fox, Bishop of Winchester, in about 1520.

The Devil swallowing Judas Iscariot. One of the few surviving wooden roof bosses from the original fifteenth century building © Southwark Cathedral

1980's Aerial view © Southwark Cathedral

The cathedral from Winchester Walk.

Remains of the Norman priory in the north aisle
© Southwark Cathedral

There are memorials to many people who have lived or worked in Southwark.

In the north choir is a statue of a knight in armour, one of the oldest wooden figures in England.

Near him is John Gower, poet and friend of Chaucer; his head is resting on his three major books, one in English, one in French and one in Latin.

There is a memorial to Shakespeare, who worked and probably lived in Southwark, erected in 1912.

Above it, a Shakespeare window, designed in 1954 to replace the earlier one destroyed in World War II, commemorates some of the characters from his plays.

Shakespeare's brother Edmund, also an actor, and the dramatists John Fletcher

The Gower tomb

and Philip Massinger are buried here, as is Lawrence Fletcher, the co-lessee of the Globe Theatre.

A modern memorial is to the fifty one victims of the "Marchioness" riverboat disaster, who drowned when the vessel sank following a collision with the dredger *Bow Belle* near Southwark Bridge on 20th August 1989.

The Marchioness memorial
© Southwark Cathedral

The Shakespeare memorial and window,
© Southwark Cathedral

The well preserved firing chamber from an 18c Delft pottery kiln at Montague Chambers, Southwark Cathedral, uncovered during excavation work in 1999. The kiln was built up against the wall of the Harvard Chapel immediately to the left. (see pages 47-49)

Southwark Cathedral.
The choir from the crossing. The elegant vaulted
space is dominated by the Fox screen (1520)
©Southwark Cathedral

St George the Martyr

The east window, showing the kneeling figure of "Little Dorrit"

There has been a church at the junction of Borough High Street and Long Lane since at least 1122, when the right to appoint the Rector was given to Bermondsey Abbey.

The present church was built in 1736, although the original bells and organ are still in use and some of the old stones from the previous building are still visible in the crypt. The present font is a copy of the old one. Registers of Births, Marriages and Deaths in the Parish from 1602 to the present day still exist. St. George's is often referred to locally as Little Dorrit's church:

> *the Dickens character was baptised and married here.*

At one time Little Dorrit lived in Marshalsea Debtors' Prison with her father. One night, returning to the prison late, she was locked out and slept in the vestry, using one of the old registers as a pillow. Her kneeling figure can be seen in the modern east window.

In 1738 when many parishes had their own local government and before tapwater was widely available, the churchwardens of St George the Martyr decided to pay £1 per year to have water from the Thames piped directly from Dockhead into a lead cistern. This cistern is still preserved within the church.

> *The Vestry was a committee which governed the parish and in 1868, decided to have the church clock lit by gas lighting. However, in order to save money, it was decided to light only three of the four faces. Electrical power is now used, but one face still remains unlit.*

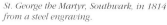

St. George the Martyr, Southwark, in 1814 from a steel engraving.

Detail from the ornate ceiling designed by Basil Champneys in 1897. It was renewed after W.W. II bomb damage and shows the Glory of God breaking through the clouds.

Winchester Palace

The 12 ft. Rose Window, Winchester Palace

*I*n medieval times, many powerful religious men had riverside estates in London. The Bishop of Rochester's property was on the site of Borough Market. To the east of London Bridge were the residences of the Prior of Lewes, the Abbot of St. Augustine's, Canterbury and the Abbot of Battle, Sussex, along with the palace of Edward II. Another estate up-river was the Manor of Paris Garden, named after Robert de Paris who lived there in the time of Richard II.

Winchester Palace, from the 1140s to 1626, was the London residence of the Bishop of Winchester.

The estate was large, with sheep, cows and pike gardens (to supply the Bishop with fresh fish), a granary for storing corn and a mill.

In those days Bishops were not only clergymen, but also great statesmen with much influence. From the river stairs at the end of Stoney Street, the Bishop could go by boat to the King's Court at Westminster.

In 1424 Cardinal Beaufort's niece Joan, married King James I of Scotland at St Mary Overie's Church (now Southwark Cathedral) The wedding feast was held in the Great Hall.

During the Commonwealth (1649 - 1660) Winchester Palace was used by Parliament as a prison for Royalist captives.

It was later used for housing and industry until 1814 when most was destroyed by fire. What survived was built into warehouses, although the west wall of the Great Hall, with its 14th century Rose Window, was saved. Modern Winchester Square

Winchester Palace from the northwe after the fire of 28th August, 18

still mirrors the shape of the inner courtyard of the Palace. Bankside is the road which ran along the river wall, built to protect the Bishop's manor against flooding and built up with twenty-two inns.

The Bishop's manor was outside the jurisdiction of the City of London or other authorities.

The Bishop, therefore, had his own court and his own prison known as The Clink, a name which has entered common usage as a term for prisons everywhere.

20

The Rose window which in the 14th century dominated the west wall of the Great Hall.

Elizabethan Southwark

*I*n Elizabethan times Southwark became the playground of the City of London; as it was outside the control of the City authorities, activities otherwise frowned upon could take place here.

The area known as Bankside in particular became known as a place of entertainment; four theatres were built here and the area was the equivalent of the modern West End.

Those who lived in the City would visit Bankside by coming over London Bridge, or alternatively by ferry, paying the ferryman one penny to travel either to St Mary Overie's Stairs, Bank End Stairs or Paris Garden Stairs, for example.

The Rose, Globe, and Bear baiting theatres, circa 1612

The Theatres

Th*he Rose Theatre was built in 1587 by Philip Henslowe, and it is known that two of Shakespeare's early plays, Titus Andronicus and Henry VI, were performed here. The Rose also saw the first performances of Christopher Marlowe's Dr. Faustus, Tamburlaine the Great and The Jew of Malta.*

Edward Alleyn, who was married to Philip Henslowe's step-daughter, was the leading actor at the Rose. There is a story that while Alleyn was playing the title role of Doctor Faustus, in his scene with the Seven Deadly Sins, he saw one too many devils on the stage with him. This experience prompted him, in 1605, to set up The College of God's Gift, now known as Dulwich College, which has in its archive many of Marlowe's papers and documents. From these it is clear that in 1592 Henslowe spent over £105 on repairs to the Rose. This was a great deal of money to be spent on 'suche charges as I have layd owt a bowte my playe howsse'. When the site of the Rose Theatre was excavated in 1989 and its foundations uncovered, it was discovered that the Rose had been considerably enlarged which would account for such great expense.

In 1605 Henslowe's lease ran out and the Rose was demolished soon after.

Before the excavation of the Rose the only surviving evidence about the interior of these theatres was a sketch by Johannes de Witt showing the inside of the Swan. The findings at the Rose have provided much needed information about the way in which Elizabethan and Jacobean theatres were constructed. At the time of the excavation, a vigorous campaign was set up to prevent the Rose from being destroyed. Subsequently the Rose Theatre Trust was formed with the aim of ensuring that the remains are put

on display to the public in the basement of the new office block on the site.

In 1999 a temporary exhibition opened, employing a sound and light show which capitalised on the subterranean-like atmosphere within the enclosed space.

The aim is to eventually re-excavate, conserve and permanently display the complete foundations of this great playhouse of Elizabethan England.

The Swan

The Swan was built in 1594 by Francis Langley in Paris Garden, west of what is now Hopton Street. Johannes de Witt wrote in 1596:

'that of all the theatres, the largest and most distinguished is that whereof the sign is a Swan'.

This playhouse did not have a regular company of actors and was sometimes used for fencing matches. After Langley's death in 1601 it was rarely used.

The last record of it was in 1632.

The Swan theatre circa 1614

Memorial to Sam Wanamaker, situated next to the Shakespeare memorial in Southwark Cathedral

Employing Elizabethan building techniques and replica tools, the Globe has been re-constructed from English oak.

The Globe

The Globe was built in 1599 using timbers from the first playhouse in Shoreditch.

The Globe was much larger than previous theatres, holding around 3,000 people, and was the first to be built by a playing company of actors with funds largely supplied by its own members.

The 'sharers' in the Globe were the eight leading players of the Lord Chamberlain's Men who included William Shakespeare. The site of the Globe is commemorated by a plaque on a wall on Park Street, close to the bridge: 'Here stood the Globe Playhouse of Shakespeare'.

A performance of 'The Winter's Tale'

The first Globe Theatre burned down in 1613 when cannon, fired during a performance of Shakespeare's Henry VIII, set fire to the thatched roof. Everyone escaped unhurt except for one man who had ' his breeches on fire that would perhaps have broyled him if he had not with the benefit of a provident wit put it out with bottle ale.' The theatre was rebuilt with a tiled roof and existed until all the playhouses were closed in 1642 by the Puritans. It was demolished two years later.

During excavations in 1989 on the original site of the Globe, some remains were discovered, although not enough has yet been found to give precise evidence about its design.

Due to the inspiration and determination of Sam Wanamaker, the American actor and director, the Globe has now been reconstructed on a site on New Globe Walk. It stands near the Thames and about two hundred metres from the original Theatre.

A performance of 'Henry V'

The Hope

The Hope was opened after the first Globe burned down, and was converted by Philip Henslowe from the former bear and bull baiting arena. It had a stage which could be removed so that bear baiting could still be held.

In 1614 Ben Jonson's Bartholomew Fair was first performed here, but after 1616 there is no record of plays being staged and it is probable that it reverted to a baiting arena.

It was dismantled in 1656.

Its approximate site is marked by the alley named Bear Gardens.

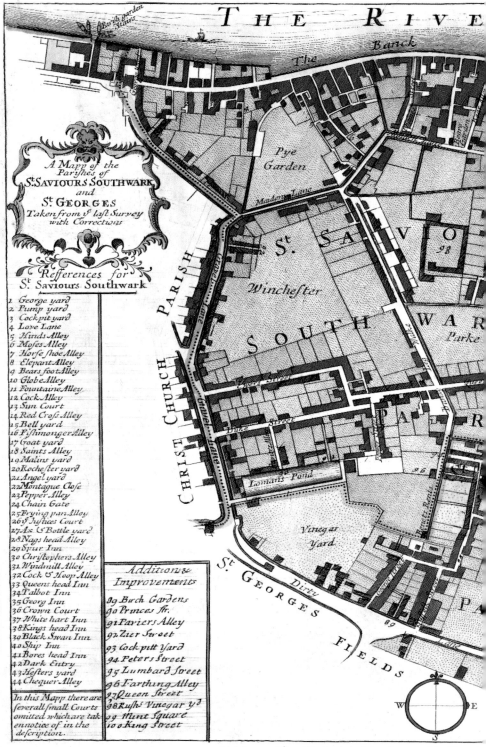

A Mapp of the
Parishes of
St SAVIOURS SOUTHWARK
and
St GEORGES
Taken from ye last Survey
with Corrections

Refferences for
St Saviours Southwark

1. George yard
2. Pump yard
3. Cockpit yard
4. Love Lane
5. Hinds Alley
6. Moses Alley
7. Horse shoe Alley
8. Elephant Alley
9. Bears foot Alley
10. Globe Alley
11. Fountaine Alley
12. Cock Alley
13. Sun Court
14. Red Cross Alley
15. Bell yard
16. Fishmonger Alley
17. Goat yard
18. Saints Alley
19. Malins yard
20. Rochester yard
21. Angel yard
22. Montague Close
23. Pepper Alley
24. Chain Gate
25. Frying pan Alley
26. ye Justices Court
27. Ax & Bottle yard
28. Nags head Alley
29. Spur Inn
30. Christophers Alley
31. Windmill Alley
32. Cock & Hoop Alley
33. Queens head Inn
34. Talbot Inn
35. Georg Inn
36. Crown Court
37. White hart Inn
38. Kings head Inn
39. Black Swan Inn
40. Ship Inn
41. Bores head Inn
42. Dark Entry
43. Hesters yard
44. Chequer Alley

In this Mapp there are
severall small Courts
omitted which are tak-
ennotice of in the
description.

Additions &
Improvements

89. Burch Gardens
90. Princes ftr.
91. Paviers Alley
92. Zier Street
93. Cockpitt Yard
94. Peters Street
95. Lumbard Street
96. Farthing Alley
97. Queen Street
98. Rushs Vinegar yd
99. Mint Square
100. King Street

THE RIVE

The Banck

Burch garden Stairs

Pye Garden

Maden Lane

St SAVO

Winchester

SOUTH WAR

Parke

CHRIST CHURCH PARISH

Cliver Street

Duke Street

Lomans Pond

Vinegar Yard

St GEORGES FIELDS

Dirty

PA

W E
S

24 *The parish of St Saviour's and part of St Georges*

St Olaves Church

Refferences for St Georges Parish

45 Windmill Alley
46 White Horse Inn
47 Gray Hound Inn
48 May Pole Alley
49 Dagger Alley
50 Red Crofs Alley
51 George Alley
52 Faulcon Court
53 Maiden head yard
54 Rose Alley
55 Ax yard
56 Bear foot Alley
57 Great yard
58 Rock yard
59 Unicorn Alley
60 Red Crofs Alley
61 Lumber Court
62 White Horse Alley
63 Crofs Shovell Alley
64 Lamb Alley
65 Dolphin yard
66 Katherin wheel yard
67 Griffin Alley
68 Black Spredd Eagle Alley
69 Three Arrow Alley
70 Maermaid Alley
71 Blew maid Alley
72 Halfe Moon Inn
73 Golden Lyon Court
74 Kings Bench Alley
75 Angel Alley
76 Golden Lyon Court
77 Shaws Court
78 Three Tun Alley
79 Baldwins Court
80 Fryingpan Alley
81 Crofs Keys Alley
82 Griffen Inn
83 White Horse Alley
84 Red Bull Alley
85 Royall Oak Court
86 Harris yard
87 Red Lyon yard
88 White Bear Alley

A Scale of Feete
100   200   300   400   500

Bankside Inns

Cardinal's Wharf, 49, Bankside

Throughout the medieval period, there were twenty-two inns situated along the length of Bankside.

The Cardinal's Cap

The Cardinal's Cap was probably named after Cardinal Wolsey who was Bishop of Winchester from 1529 to 1530. Actors from the Bankside theatres were known to have met here. Cardinal Cap Alley, which still exists, led to the inn, and Cardinal's Wharf (49 Bankside) was built on the site around 1700.

This building is a rare survivor of many similar houses on Bankside.

On the side of the building a plaque reads 'Here lived Christopher Wren during the building of St Paul's Cathedral', but this is considered most unlikely, the area at that time hardly being in keeping with a man of Wren's status.

Fanciful too is the story that in 1502, Catharine, Infanta of Castile and Aragon, took shelter here on her way to meet Henry VIII, whose first Queen she became.

These stories began in about 1950 when one Malcolm Munthe, son of Axel Munthe, Swedish author of 'The story of San Michele', occupied the property. Various items such as finials, coats of arms and shields appeared which lent a certain historical significance to the property which, for the most part, is largely unfounded.

The Falcon

The Falcon was a large riverside inn, marked now by Falcon Point, a block of flats near Blackfriars Bridge.

From an inn on Bankside in September 1666 Samuel Pepys watched the Great Fire of London.

Later, in 1668, he wrote in his diary: 'by water over to Southwark and so walked to the Falcon on Bankside ...'.

The Anchor

The only remaining inn on Bankside from around this period is The Anchor, built in 1775 on the site of an older inn called the Castle on the Hoop. Previously used as a tavern, a brothel, a coffee house, a chapel, a brewery and a ship's chandlers. Dr. Johnson is said to have written his dictionary here in rooms rented from Mrs. Thrale, the landlady. Other notable visitors include Boswell and the artist, Joshua Reynolds.

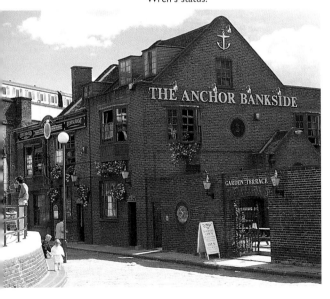

The Anchor, Bankside

Stews, Bear & Bull Baiting

The inns of Bankside were also known as Stews, another name for the brothels which were prevalent in this vicinity.

As this area came under the jurisdiction of the Bishop of Winchester, the prostitutes who worked in the brothels were consequently known as 'Winchester Geese'.

Stew Lane, across the river in the City, was an embarkation point for the women travelling to their place of business on Bankside.

The Stews were closed down by Henry VIII in 1546.

Bear-baiting. A cruel but popular sport

Bear and bull baiting

A popular entertainment here since medieval times was the horrific pastime of bear and bull baiting.

The animal was tied to a stake and set upon by dogs.

Queen Elizabeth I is known to have brought the French ambassador by barge to watch the bear baiting. In 1604 Edward Alleyn was made Master of the Royal Bears, Bulls and Mastiff Dogs.

The last Bear Garden was closed in 1682.

" TO PLAIE V DOGGES AT THE SINGLE BEARE FOR V POUNDS"
An ancient manuscript advertisement from the old Bankside bear garden

Below: *Bankside Southwark in 1648 with a view of "Hollands Leaguer"- one of the ancient "stews" or licensed brothels there*

Geoffrey Chaucer

Literary Southwark

Over the years, Southwark has been associated with some of the greatest writers in the English language.

Geoffrey Chaucer (1345?-1400)

Geoffrey Chaucer is best known for his 'Canterbury Tales', written around 1387, and particularly interesting for the vivid picture it presents of contemporary life. It describes a party of thirty-one pilgrims, including Chaucer himself, who assemble at the Tabard Inn in Southwark, and travel to the shrine of St Thomas Becket at Canterbury. After supper on the first night it was suggested that, to shorten the journey, each of the pilgrims should tell two stories on the way to Canterbury and two on the way back. Chaucer died before completing the work which contains only twenty-three tales. Chaucer is known to have gone on pilgrimage to Canterbury in April 1388.

He was buried in Westminster Abbey, but not until 1555 was a monument erected to him

Charles Dickens

both an actor and playwright, and a member of a company of players known as the Lord Chamberlain's Men.

In 1599 he was involved with that company's establishment of the Globe Theatre.

Shakespeare had already written many of his plays by the time the Globe was built, but his greatest plays, Hamlet, Othello, Macbeth and King Lear were all written for this playhouse. He bought New Place in Stratford in 1597, by which time he was apparently a wealthy man, although he did not settle there permanently until 1611, and died there five years later. Most of Shakespeare's plays were collected together by two of his fellow actors, Heminge and Condell, and published in 1623. There is a memorial to Shakespeare and a Shakespeare window in Southwark Cathedral .

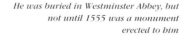

William Shakespeare (1564-1616)

William Shakespeare was born in Stratford upon Avon and spent his early life there;

He is usually associated with this town even though Southwark was the place where he spent most of his working life.

He left Stratford in about 1585 and was next heard of in London. He was probably involved with the two earliest theatres in London, the Theatre and the Curtain. By 1592 he was established as

The Globe Theatre c.1612, in the reign of James

William Shakespeare

28

Charles Dickens (1812-70)

Charles Dickens knew Southwark very well and particularly the area known as the Borough, the neighbourhood of Borough High Street.

His early life was in some ways similar to those experiences depicted in his book 'David Copperfield'

and his vivid descriptions of the area provide useful information about 19th century Southwark . His family, which had led a comfortable, middle-class existence, had a change of fortune in 1824 when

Charles's father was imprisoned in the Marshalsea, a debtors' prison.

He was joined there by Mrs Dickens and all the children except Charles and Fanny. At twelve years of age, Charles went to work in a blacking factory at Hungerford Stairs and moved into lodgings in Lant Street.

It is believed that his description of a workhouse in 'Oliver Twist' was based on the old St George's workhouse in Mint Street.

The "Dog's head in a pot" - a Southwark ironmonger's sign which Dickens used to pass each day when working at a blacking factory in his boyhood.

Water pump from Marshalsea Debtor's Prison. Dickens' father must have seen this every day of his imprisonment.

Many of Dickens' characters have been immortalised in the names of streets in the area: Weller Street, Pickwick Street, Quilp Street, Dorrit Street, Copperfield Street and Clennam Street. There are many references to Southwark in Dickens' work.

Dickens' early career was as a newspaper reporter, but went on to write a series of articles for journals. The first collection was subsequently published as 'Sketches by Boz'. His more famous novels were often produced in this way, and included Oliver Twist, Nicholas Nickleby and Little Dorrit.

In 1842 Dickens went to America, where he advocated international copyright and the abolition of slavery. In 1858 Dickens started giving public readings from his books, which he continued during his second visit to America in 1867-8. After his return to England he started writing Edwin Drood, but died suddenly before its completion.

John Harvard (1607-1638)

*P*rincipal benefactor and namesake of Harvard University USA, John Harvard was born in Southwark in 1607.

Plaque on the site of the Queen's Head Inn Borough High Street, which was owned by John Harvard's mother, Katherine and is currently occupied by a firm of solicitors.

John's father was a butcher and Inn-Keeper in Borough High Street and died in the plague, along with four of his brothers and sisters in 1625.

Christened at St Saviour's Church, (now Southwark Cathedral) John attended St Saviour's Grammar School before being sent to to Emmanuel College, Cambridge in 1627, where he finally received his masters degree in 1635.

His mother, Katherine, later bought the Queen's Head Inn in Borough High Street and subsequently bequeathed it to John.

Later, he decided to sell the inn and start a new life in America with his newlywed wife Ann. They settled in Charlestown where the first English colonies were being founded, arriving there in 1637 with over 400 books on a variety of subjects, including religion and grammar together with assorted Latin and Greek texts.

He soon became a Freeman of the town, and served as assistant pastor to the First Church of Charlestown.

He died the following year at the age of thirty, but he left 'one half of his estate towards the erecting of a college, and all his library'.

At the behest of Massachusetts General Court in 1639, this college became known as Harvard University which has not forgotten the roots of its benefactor.

The Harvard Chapel in Southwark Cathedral was restored with donations from the Friends of Harvard University.

The Harvard Chapel in Southwark Cathedral. © Southwark Cathedral

The Pugin Tabernacle © Southwark Cathedral

From an etching of Southwark Cathedral in 1885

ENGLISH ETCHINGS, PART IX.

The Prisons

Southwark was renowned for its gaols, of which there were six altogether, and which housed wrong-doers from all over London.

Replaced in 2003, this plaque in Clink Street testifies to the historic significance of this part of Southwark

The prisons were probably established here because it was near to London but outside the city walls. Conditions were appalling and there was horrendous overcrowding.

Prisoners could die of starvation as they were expected to beg for food from passers by.

Imprisonment was not the normal punishment for the general run of criminal offences; physical punishment and transportation were usual. In the 16th and 17th centuries the prisons also housed those whose religious beliefs differed from the ruler of the day.

Horsemonger Lane Gaol

Many were used as debtors' prisons, and those who were so confined might have stayed there unless and until someone could bail them out. The most notorious of the prisons were:

The Marshalsea

The Marshalsea was an old prison whose name is derived from an ancient court held by the Knight Marshal of the King's Household. The date of its establishment is unknown but it was attacked by Wat Tyler's rebels in 1381.

Under Elizabeth I it became one of the most important of London's prisons, second only to the Tower. It was mainly used for debtors;

Charles Dicken's father was imprisoned here for that reason in 1824.

The Marshalsea was closed in 1842; pictured below is the one remaining brick wall of the old prison which can still be seen alongside the Local Studies Library.

The King's Bench

The King's Bench took its name from the gaols attached to the court of King's Bench which travelled from town to town. The first prison stood on the east side of Borough High Street.

In 1554 the martyr John Bradford was imprisoned here before his execution, but the majority of prisoners were debtors.

Like the Clink, the King's Bench was burned in the Gordon Riots in 1780, but was quickly rebuilt.

In 1869 debt ceased to be an imprisonable offence and the King's Bench was used for a time as a military prison. It was demolished in 1880.

Above: *A cat and two rats, mummified in the moment of conflict, found beneath 16th century woodwork in Borough High St.*

A view of the first site of Marshalsea prison, up until 1811

The Clink

The Clink was first referred to as such in 1503, although there is evidence that a prison had existed here since medieval times. Between 1144-1149 the prison formed part of the palace of the Bishop of Winchester and was intended as a punishment for laymen and women, and offending clergy who were not subject to the jurisdiction of lay courts.

By 1473 the area surrounding Winchester Palace became known as the Liberty of the See of Winchester, under the jurisdiction of the Bishop of Winchester, who derived great income from the regulation and supervision of the brothels and inns in the vicinity. The Clink was the means by which the Bishop maintained order and imposed his authority over the more disorderly clientele.

Another feature of the Bishop's Manor was its sanctuary against civil law, (Being outside the control of the City) providing a haven for evil and distasteful characters of every type.

Torture increased with the return of the knights from the first crusade, and unspeakable treatment became commonplace. Entirely at the mercy of their keepers, prisoners were obliged to beg or to prostitute themselves in order to provide the income necessary to improve their conditions by bribing the jailers.

In 1352 debtors increased the prison's population, which provided the jailers with further scope for increasing their income by forcing inmates to pay fees for release, etc.

later on, the prison housed both Protestant and Catholic prisoners of concience. About 1580 saw a report which described the hole as a fearsome place where prisoners were left to rot.

The Clink was sacked and its inmates released more than once in its lifetime, but the Gordon Riots of 1780 finally saw an end to this appalling place when it was burned down, never to be rebuilt.

Horsemonger Lane Gaol

Horsemonger Lane Gaol, built in 1791, was further south on Borough High Street by Harper Road (once Horsemonger Lane) on the site now marked by the Newington Gardens Recreation Ground.

Public executions were held outside and it was here in November 1849 that Dickens attended a public hanging at which he was so appalled that he wrote to The Times, complaining of the 'atrocious bearing, looks and language of the assembled spectators'.

The gaol was closed in 1878 and demolished in 1880.

Clink Street, 1996

33

Thomas Guy

The Hospitals

*U*ntil 1862 St Thomas' and Guy's Hospitals faced each other across St Thomas Street, off Borough High Street. Guy's still occupies one side of St Thomas Street; St Thomas's has since moved to the riverside by Westminster Bridge.

St Thomas' Hospital

St Thomas' Hospital was founded in the early 13th century as part of the Priory of St Mary Overie. Its name, The Hospital of St Thomas the Martyr, was assumed after Becket's canonisation in 1173. It became a separate institution in 1215 after it was destroyed by fire and rebuilt in 1540 to the east of Borough High Street. During the dissolution of the monasteries, Henry VIII closed the hospital; it re-opened in 1551 as the Hospital of St Thomas the Apostle and grew into a large hospital with a church for the people of St Thomas' parish.

Inside the roof of the church - the female operating theatre discovered in 1956

After the Crimean War, Florence Nightingale founded the Nightingale Training School of Nursing here; the first such school for nurses St Thomas' nurses are still known as Nightingales.

St Thomas' Hospital was moved to make way for an extension to London Bridge Station. Only the South Wing survives today and is used by the GPO in Borough High Street. The buildings were mostly demolished, although the church survives; inside its roof is the 19th century female's operating theatre of the hospital, rediscovered in 1956, complete with the narrow wooden table where surgeons would have performed operations without the aid of anaesthetic.

The roof was also used as a herb garret, where the apothecary would have stored and mixed the herbs to be used as medicine.

The Old Operating Theatre Museum, St Thomas' Street

Guy's Hospital

Guy's Hospital was opened in 1726 by Thomas Guy, the son of a river boatman of Fair Street, Bermondsey. Guy became very wealthy, largely through clever investments, and became a governor of St Thomas'. When he realised that the older hospital could not take in all the patients needing care he used his money to build a hospital across the road.

In his will he left £220,000 to maintain Guy's.

His statue stands in the centre of the oldest part of the hospital, now much enlarged, and he is buried in the chapel.

In 1799 Guy's was the first hospital in London to appoint a dental surgeon, and it became famous for its Dental School.

It is still one of the great teaching hospitals of the world.

London Bridge, 1560

Borough High Street, 1881

Southwark's Industrial Heritage

Bas-reliefs outside the Hide and Leather Exchange, Leather Market

*L*ondon, in common with other ancient cities, was built on a river, not only for an easy supply of water but also because it meant that goods from other areas could be brought in by boat. The Thames has been used as a highway for trade since Roman times; recent excavations in Park Street uncovered the remains of a Roman warehouse, and a Roman ship was found, in what had once been an inlet of the Thames, during building work at Guy's Hospital.

Crafts and trades

During the Elizabethan period there were many workshops near the river so that craftsmen had access to the ships which brought in the raw materials.

Many of the craftsmen were immigrants or religious refugees, for example, those of Dutch or Flemish origin.

They settled in Southwark to avoid restrictions imposed by the City on newcomers who tried to set up in business in competition with the indigenous population.

Glass

Between 1515-31 an eminent group of Glaziers operated within the grounds of old St Thomas' Hospital in St Thomas Street. They made the famous stained glass windows for King's College Chapel, Cambridge.

Three members of this group held the title of King's Glazier.

Bernard Flower, Galyon Hone and Peter Nicholson. Later the area had glasshouses producing bottles, drinking vessels and glass for windows. The Glaziers Company, one of the City Livery Companies, has its headquarters at Glaziers

Hall in Montague Close, between Southwark Cathedral and the river.

Continuing the tradition of glassworking in Southwark, the London Glassblowing Workshop has achieved an international reputation for its visual style and innovative use of colour and texture. Founded by Peter Layton in 1976, the studio produces a wide variety of designs employing techniques such as sand-blasting, acid etching and metalworking. The London Glassblowing Workshop's studio is at 7, The Leathermarket, Weston St, London SE1 3ER. Telephone: 020 7403 2800

Craftsman shaping the glass with newspaper at the London Glassblowing Workshop

ral flask and bowls, de by the London ssblowing rkshop in mondsey.

37

The Leathermarket, Weston Street, Bermondsey

Leather

From the Middle Ages the chief place for the manufacture of leather was Bermondsey. Animal skins were available from the butchers of London and the process of tanning was eased by Southwark's supply of water from its many streams and rivers. Oak bark was used in the process, and there was a plentiful supply from the woods in the outlying districts of Forest Hill, Norwood and Honor Oak. The finished leather could easily be transported to the markets of the City of London. There are many echoes of the industry in the area: Tanner Street, Morocco Street, Skin Market Place, and Leathermarket Street which leads to the Leathermarket, a building erected in 1879. There is also a public house called Simon the Tanner in Long Lane.

Print

Peter Treveris, one of the earliest printers, printed a large history book called Higden's Polychronicon in 1527.

> *The first edition of The Bible was printed by James Nicholson at St Thomas' Hospital in 1537.*

Pottery

Pottery made over three hundred and fifty years ago was discovered by archaeologists in Potters Fields, west of Tower Bridge, and close to the Thames. In the 17th and early 18th centuries, the area around what is now Montague Close and adjacent to Southwark Cathedral, was an important place for the manufacture of English Delftware, (ie tin-glazed).

Excavation works in 1999 exposed these Delftware kilns, together with a Roman road leading to London Bridge and an 18th century burial shaft containing the skeletons of bodies buried one on top of the other. (see page 47)

Tin-glazed delftware with its distinctive yellow and blue colouring was extremely popular with the American colonies, and one of the largest collections can be found at Williamsburg, Virginia. © Southwark Cathedral

Buiscuitware wasters (ie pots which were rejected before being fired) from the Delft pottery kiln at Montague Chambers, Southwark Cathedral.

Sculpture

Gheerart Jannson, a Dutchman, later known as Gerald Johnson, worked as a sculptor with his five sons at a wharf just down river from London Bridge.

> *One of the Johnsons carved the figure of Lancelot Andrewes in Southwark Cathedral and another made the monument for Shakespeare's tomb at Stratford upon Avon.*

William Cure of Amsterdam and his family, who lived near St Thomas', made the memorial to Mary, Queen of Scots, in Westminster Abbey.

The Hop Exchange, Southwark Street

Hops/Brewing

The Borough was especially noted as the centre of the English hop trade. Brewing was an important industry even in the Middle Ages, especially when the finished product could be sold to those travelling to and from the City over London Bridge. In his Tale, in Chaucer's 'Canterbury Tales', the Miller refers to the local brew:

"If the words get muddled in my tale, Just put it down to too much Southwark ale".

Sacks of hops were brought from Kent, Worcester and Hereford and from abroad, to be stored in the hop merchants' warehouses. They were then sold to the brewers for making beer, notably Barclay & Perkins, a very old brewery in Park Street, and Courage's on the riverside in Bermondsey, east of Tower Bridge, founded in 1787.

In 1866 the Hop and Malt Exchange was built, in Southwark Street, with a glass roof so that the quality of the hops could be examined by natural light. The Hop Exchange was recently refurbished, although it is not now used for its original purpose. In 1955 Barclay & Perkins was amalgamated with Courage's, which closed both its local factories in the 1980s.

Barclay & Perkins' brewery 1841

39

Southwark's Docks &Wharves

*B**y the middle of the 18th century the river trade on the
Thames had been considerably developed. For over one
hundred years, until the early 1970s, the Southwark river
front was lined with tall warehouses similar to those which still
overshadow part of Clink Street. Goods were brought in by barge,
unloaded by cranes, and stored in the warehouses until they were
taken to their various destinations.*

*Hays Wharf 2003, or Hays
Galleria as it is now
known, is a superb under-
cover space surrounded by
shops, restaurants and
market stalls.*

*Below: low tide at St
Saviour's Dock*

In 1831, a new London Bridge was built
which had wider arches, making it
possible for barges to get further up river.
Bankside became especially busy and
many new warehouses were built.

> *Pickfords Wharf in Clink Street is now
> converted into an apartment block, but it
> was originally built in 1864 for the storage
> of flour, hops and seeds.*

Many factories were built in Southwark
because the raw materials could be
brought by river, and new road and rail
links made it easier to transport the
finished goods.

The area down river from London Bridge
right up to Bermondsey was known as
London's Larder; three-quarters of the
butter, bacon, cheese and canned meat
needed for London was stored here.

The Hay's Wharf Company owned many
of the warehouses, and Alexander Hay,
who founded the company in 1651, took
over some property near the small inlet
of the Thames now known as Hay's
Galleria. When these buildings were
destroyed by Southwark's great fire in
1676, Alexander's son Joseph set up a
fire insurance scheme with his neighbours
called 'Ye Amicable Contributors'.

> *In 1861 another conflagration, the Great
> Fire of Tooley Street, raged in the area for
> two weeks causing damage estimated to
> cost over £2 million. The fire began in
> Cotton's Wharf. Sugar, rice and cotton
> ignited, producing a lava-like mass which
> flowed onto the Thames, setting fire to the
> wooden ships moored there. These blazing
> hulks broke free of their moorings, drifted
> downstream causing more fires to break
> out elsewhere.*

New warehouses were built in 1856 and
Hay's Wharf, where cold storage was
pioneered, continued to prosper. The
area was heavily bombed during the
Second World War and many of the
docks were very badly damaged. They
were rebuilt after the war,

> *but by the 1970s this period of London's
> history had come to an end.*

The need for deeper docks for container
ships grew and the wharves in the centre
of London were all closed. Many of the

*Hay's Wharf: Now a Thameside
walk with shops and restaurants*

Cotton's Wharf ablaze, where the great fire of Tooley Street began in 1861. © Fire Brigade museum

old warehouses have been demolished or converted; Hay's Wharf became Hay's Galleria, a showplace for shops and restaurants.

Borough Market

Also known as 'London's Larder' Borough Market has an illustrious history going back at least until 1276, from which time a street market selling all sorts of goods was held on the old London Bridge. It is said to be one of the oldest fruit and vegetable market in Britain. In 1756, due to the chaos and traffic congestion, the market was moved off the highway and re-established selling just fruit and vegetables in buildings designed by H Rose in 1851. Borough and Smithfield Markets are the only wholesale markets still remaining in central London; all others have been moved to the outskirts of the city.

The market's fortunes have recently revived becoming a popular attraction specializing in organic foods, fresh fruit, meat, cheeses and vegetables and is open on Fridays and Saturdays.

Bourough Market

Tea and coffee

China was the principal source of tea imports into the U.K from 1660, but by 1900 had mostly given way to tea from India and Ceylon producers.

Tea and coffee has been traded and warehoused at Butlers Wharf for 350 years, and during its heyday could certainly have handled 5,000-6,000 chests of tea in a single day. These cargoes would have been unloaded further downstream and transported up river to Butlers Wharf by lighter.

The Bramah Tea and Coffee Museum is situated in Southwark Street near Borough Market and houses a fine collection of tea and coffee artefacts from around the world. Visitors are invited to enjoy freshly made beverages and pastries in the tea room, or choose from a variety of items including fresh tea, coffee, and memorabilia which are on sale in the shop.

Top right: Grocers sign made in papier maché, early 20th century. middle: Barge teapot commemorating fifty years of the reign of Queen Victoria, 1887. Bottom: Chinese porcelain, Quianlong teapot with silver lid, c.1740

Hay's Wharf c. 1857

Schools

*T**he oldest schools in Southwark were St Olave's Grammar School founded in 1561 and St Saviour's Grammar School, founded in 1562.**

The original seal, showing a robed schoolmaster seated at a table with birch and book, and five pupils.

The first schools were founded for the parishioners of St Olave's and St Saviour's Churches, which were located either side of the southern end of London Bridge.

St Saviour's was the first of the two schools to receive a Charter from Queen Elizabeth I in 1562, Followed by St Olave's in 1571.

Among the first Governors of St Saviour's were Thomas Cure, Saddler to Queen Elizabeth; Robert Harvard, whose son John was probably a pupil at St Saviour's and who was later to found Harvard University; and Philip Henslowe, the Elizabethan theatre manager.

An early Headmaster was Robert Browne, founder of Congregationalism and reputedly Shakespeare's model for Malvolio in 'Twelfth Night'.

St Olave's Grammar School from 1849-1968 at the southern end of Tower Bridge, in Tooley Street.

The construction of the London-Greenwich railway necessitated a re-location to a neo-Tudor building by James Field, in Bermondsey Street in 1835.

Following further widening of the railway, in 1849 the school again moved, this time to a building at the foot of Tower Bridge.

In 1896, St Olave's and St Saviour's were amalgamated.

The boys' school became St Olave's Grammar School, which relocated to Orpington, Kent, in 1968. The girls' school, St Saviour's and St Olave's opened its current building in New Kent Road in 1903.

St Olave's Grammar School 1835-1849, by James Field

Fire Brigade

*Memorial to James
Braidwood, Cottons Lane*

***B**efore there was a centralised service, fires were dealt with by small fire-fighting squads organised by insurance companies.*

Those owners who insured their property would have a Fire Mark, a metal badge, to fix to their outside wall.

Each company had its own fire mark;

if the one displayed was not its own, the fire-fighting squad would leave the property to burn. In 1833 the London Fire Engine Establishment was set up, under Superintendent James Braidwood, who was killed during the Great Fire of Tooley Street in 1861. A memorial to him can be seen high on the wall in Cotton's Lane off Tooley Street.

As a direct result of the Great Fire, the Metropolitan Fire Brigade (which later became the London Fire Brigade in 1904) was founded in 1866 with Captain Eyre Massey Shaw as its Superintendent.

Superintendent James Braidwood

Captain Shaw lived at Winchester House, in Southwark Bridge Road, which, from 1878 until 1937, was the Headquarters of the London Fire Brigade. It is now the London Fire Brigade Museum, housing the most fascinating collection of fire-fighting equipment and memorabilia to be seen anywhere in the world.

*Two-man manual pump
in use around 1740*

*London's Fire Brigade
Museum situated in
Winchester House,
Southwark Bridge Road*

Bankside ~ *the regeneration*

Tate Modern is housed in a former power station designed by Giles Gilbert Scott. It was converted by Swiss architects Herzog and de Meuron and opened in May 2000.

Bankside is one of the oldest settlements in Britain and evidence of human habitation dates back to the Neolithic period over 6000 years ago.

At that time, the Thames was much shallower and wider than it is today. When the Romans founded Londinium on the north bank of the Thames, they chose as their crossing point a site close to the present day London Bridge and the area south and west of this point has been inhabited ever since. However, due to the area being low lying and marshy only land close to the river bank itself was originally settled.

This area has provided London with a site for various activities not always welcomed in the City itself. Over the years it has been a home to prisoners, prostitutes, gamblers, drinkers and other 'undesirables'.

It was through its role as an Elizabethan 'red light' district that Bankside developed into London's first theatre district. Some of England's greatest writers and players lived and worked here, most notably William Shakespeare.

Despite its proximity to the City, Bankside remained a largely rural enclave right up until the late eighteenth century when it quickly developed into an industrial and urban environment and the riverside became lined with docks,

warehouses and wharves. Following industrial decline after the Second World War, Bankside remained largely undiscovered until its renaissance as one of the capital's prime visitor destinations began with the reconstruction of Shakespeare's Globe, the Millennium Bridge and Tate Modern.

Shakespeare's Globe completed in 1997.

Extensively refurbished railway arches adjacent to the thames are home to Vinopolis, a unique attraction offering a tour of the world's major wine growing regions. The informative tour provides an insight into the world of wine and plenty of tasting opportunities.

Vinopolis.
A wine tour of the world under the railway arches.

The Millennium Bridge. Planned as the first new bridge to span the Thames during the 20th century, it opened briefly in 2000 but closed within a few days due to a severe lateral 'sway' caused by the huge crowds passing along it. A series of dampers were devised as a counter measure and the bridge re-opened in 2002.

Below: Bankside 2002.
Photos: Nik Milner.
Photo-montage, Robert Godley

Archaeology ~ *discovering a hidden legacy*

*N*orth Southwark is currently undergoing a process of development and regeneration. Derelict land, empty buildings and unused docks and wharves represented the end of an historic era of intensive industrial, trading and commercial usage.

The redevelopment of the land and conversion of buildings has brought new life to the area in the form of housing and offices, transport services, entertainment and cultural activities.

It is this very process of development which is bringing new archaeological and historical discoveries to light, not just from the recent industrial past but also from distant prehistory.

During the prehistoric period much of North Southwark consisted of sandy islands along a much wider River Thames. Typically the oldest sites have consisted of camps for the probable seasonal exploitation of the islands, i.e. fowl hunting, fishing and plant gathering, and the finds have been flint tools and pieces of flint burnt and cracked during cooking. While the exploitation of the land margins continued, Bronze Age period sites at Hopton Street and St Saviour's Dock have shown the ploughing of land using the primitive ard (plough). Actual prehistoric settlement sites have now been found at Swan Street, off Borough High Street, and most recently at Three Oak Lane, off Tooley Street, where, as well as gullies and postholes, a redundant wooden ard share was found in the backfill of a ditch.

Right: Archaeologists working across the prehistoric, Roman and Post-Medieval site of Swan Street off Borough High Street.

Roman pots which were deliberately broken and placed within a timber lined well at Swan Street off Borough High Street, probably as part of a ritual.

Much Roman archaeology has been found around the junction of the main Roman roads of Stane Street and Watling Street, near the present site of St George the Martyr, and northwards along Borough High Street to the bridgehead, near the present London Bridge. These roads as well as networks of smaller roads, ditches and revetted channels have shown the massive infrastructure investments of the Roman period. Vast amounts of earth, domestic and industrial rubbish was dumped in wet areas during much of the first three centuries AD to reclaim marshy land. Both masonry and clay and timber buildings have been found along the roads while the waste from various industrial activities has been found in pits and ditches.

45

The archaeological excavation of warehouses and earlier domestic buildings at West Courtyard Butlers Wharf.

The remains of deliberately broken pots in a disused well and the upper part of a man's skeleton and a dog skull in another well, may have been placed there as part of rituals.

Further investigations have been undertaken at the site of Medieval Bermondsey Abbey (Bermondsey Market) and the above and below ground remains of the priory of St Mary Overie (Southwark Cathedral). Other Medieval remains have been found at the Millenium Bridge and Adlards Wharf on Bermondsey Wall West, where timber river revetments dating from the 14th to 19th centuries have been excavated.

Some of the most interesting recent discoveries in Southwark have been from the Post-Medieval and Industrial ages. From the 17th century onwards expansion of industry, shipping and trade, together with the supporting population growth, resulted in the rapid spread of the urban centre. Development took place along the river edge, along Shad Thames and Bermondsey Wall West, and along roadways, such as Bermondsey Street.

Gradually the wetter land between these ribbons of settlement was raised using huge quantities of dumped waste and the resultant land was built over.

Both the waste material and the structures of the land reclamation enables us to see some local activities, such as broken and unfinished pottery from local production and timbers from ship-breaking being reused in river revetments.

In particular reclamation was undertaken in the Butlers Wharf area on a massive scale and the

Archaeologists at work in a Roman roadside ditch at Southwark Cathedral. The timber stakes visible to the right were to support and consolidate the road which headed towards the Roman London Bridge.

Skeletons from an 18th century burial shaft at Southwark Cathedral. All these individuals were buried in coffins in a single shaft, which remained open until filled, and which has subsequently slumped due to decomposition and compaction.

present day grid-pattern of the streets represents units of land which were settled along the edges first while the central areas were reclaimed. In this area archaeological excavations have uncovered warehouses, houses and factories, and while Butlers Wharf has undergone many changes it remains one of the best preserved commercial landscapes in the country.

Other industrial activities have been examined archaeologically, including a whale processing centre at Greenland Docks, Rotherhithe, where massive whale bones were found reused in dock construction. The widespread leather tanning industry is often found in the form of wooden tanning pits, especially in the areas near Long Lane and Tower Bridge Road, and has even been found to date back to the Medieval period at Tanner Street. Kilns for the manufacturing of 17th and 18th century Delft pottery have been found at Southwark Cathedral, Bear Gardens and at the Pickle Herring

Brick firing chamber for a whale blubber rendering cauldron, and wooden tank for rendered oil at Greenland Docks, Rotherhithe.

potteries between London Bridge and Tower Bridge. Furnaces for the manufacturing of glass from the mid 1700's and from Apsley Pellatt's early 19th century Falcon Glassworks have been excavated at Hopton Street and glass production has also been found at Ben Bow House, Bankside. The processes and history of vinegar production and spice grinding have been recorded in buildings prior to their conversions at Roper Street and Butlers Wharf.

View over excavations of Roman riverside activity at Hunts House, Guy's Hospital, towards Borough High Street.

Excavations of timber revetments at Adlards Wharf (Bermondsey Wall West) which reclaimed land from the River Thames, progressively from the right (Medieval) to left (19th century). Most of the timbers were reused from salvaged ships and boats.

Bibliography and Local Organisations

- Charles Dickens and Southwark, London Borough of Southwark, Library Services
- Documents of the Rose Playhouse, Carol Chillington Rutter
- The London Encyclopaedia, Ben Weinreb and Christopher Hibbert
- Rescuing the past in Southwark – Southwark and Lambeth Archaeological Excavation Committee
- The Rose Theatre: Past Present and Future, Museum of London
- Rebuilding Shakespeare's Globe by Andrew Gurr with John Orrell
- Square Mile Walks: Six Walks in the City of London, Belinda Morse
- The Story of Bankside, London Borough of Southwark, Neighbourhood Histories
- The Story of Bermondsey, London Borough of Southwark, Neighbourhood Histories
- The Story of the Borough, London Borough of Southwark, Neighbourhood Histories
- Two Schools: A History of St Olave's & St Saviour's Grammar School Foundation, R C Carrington, 1971

Local Organisations Associated with Southwark's Heritage

- The Anchor, 1 Bankside, London SE1 Tel (020) 7407 1577
- Bramah Tea and Coffee Museum, 40 Southwark St, London SE1. Tel (020) 7403 5650
- Corporation of London, Guildhall, London EC2 Tel (020) 7606 3030
- The Clink Exhibition, Clink Street, London SE1 Tel (020) 7403 0900
- Dulwich College, Dulwich, London SE21 Tel (020) 8693 3601
- The George Inn, 77 Borough High Street, London SE1 Tel (020) 7407 2056
- Glaziers Hall, 9 Montague Close, London SE1 Tel (020) 7407 3300
- Guy's Hospital, St Thomas Street, London SE1 Tel (020) 7955 5000

- Hay's Galleria: St Martins Property Corporation Ltd, 1 Battlebridge Lane, London, SE1 2HP Tel: (020) 7403 3583
- Local Studies Library, Angel Court, Borough High Street, London S E1 Tel: (020) 7403 3507
- London Fire Brigade Museum, Winchester House, Southwark Bridge Road, London SE1 Tel (020) 7587 2894
- Museum of London, London Wall, London, EC2Y 5HN Tel (020) 7600 1058
- Old Operating Theatre Museum, 9a St Thomas' Street, London SE1 Tel (020) 7955 4791
- Pre-Construct Archaeology Limited, Unit 54 Brockley Cross Business Centre, London, SE4 2PD Tel (020) 7639 9091
- Rose Theatre Trust, 2 Rose Alley, London SE1 9AS Tel (020) 7593 0026 Fax (020) 7633 0367
- Shakespeare's Globe Exhibition, New Globe Walk, London SE1 9DT Tel (020) 7902 1500
- Southwark Cathedral, Montague Close, London SE1 Tel (020) 7367 6700
- Southwark Heritage Association, 216 Upland Rd, London SE22 ODJ Tel (020) 8299 0470
- St George's Cathedral, Southwark, London SE1 Tel (020) 7940 5256
- St George the Martyr, Borough High Street, London SE1
- Tower Bridge, London SE1 2UP Tel (020) 7940 3985
- Vinopolis City of Wine Bank End London SE1 9BU Tel (020) 7940 8300